Introducti

When you look at the next page, you'll see a fly lo... been magnified a hundred times so you can get a r... will look alive in 3D.

3D images included in this title shown below in miniature.

Earwig

Dust Mite

Mosquito

Jumping Spider

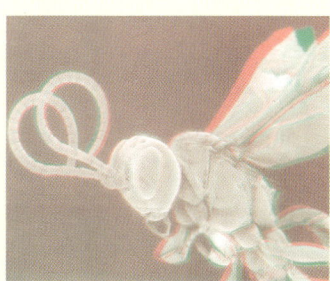
Ichneumon

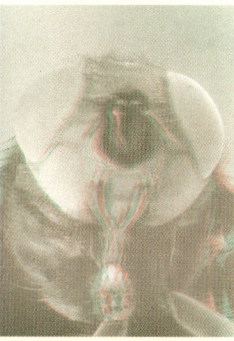
House Fly

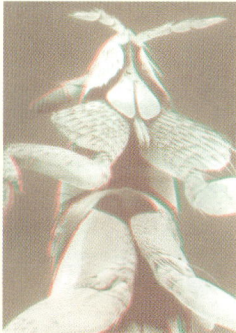
Flea

Pea Beetle

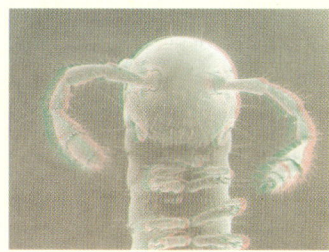
Millipede

Cricket

Springtail

Author: Chris Madsen
Development: Martin Rhodes-Schofield
Specialist 3D Photography: David Burder

First Published 1998   Second Edition 2000   Third Edition 2002

Red Bird Publishing © 1998
Brightlingsea, Colchester CO7 0SX, England.

Origination, Special Effects and Production:
Technographic, Halesworth, Suffolk IP19 8QJ, England.

Flies

Mayfly larva
Mayflies only fly for a day. Their larvae live in ponds and streams. This larva's three leaf-shaped 'tails' are gills.

Hoverfly
A hoverfly's striking resemblance to a wasp helps to keep it safe from birds. Among the gardener's friends, these flies eat many pests, such as greenflies.

Horsefly
Male horseflies feed on plant juices. Only the females are bloodsuckers. They can land secretly, but their bite is a sharp, stabbing pain.

FACT FILE

House Fly

Houseflies are high on the list of hazards in the home. Their feet carry germs from rotting garbage to food on a plate, and the way they feed adds more germs. Because these flies have no jaws, they can only take in liquid food. The hollow tongue has two jobs: first it drops digestive juices onto the food, and then it sucks up the liquefied result.

A fly's eyes give it an excellent view of the world around it. They are known as 'compound' eyes because each is made up of many smaller eyes. The picture of the world a fly sees may resemble the large picture produced by a bank of TV screens at an outdoor pop concert.

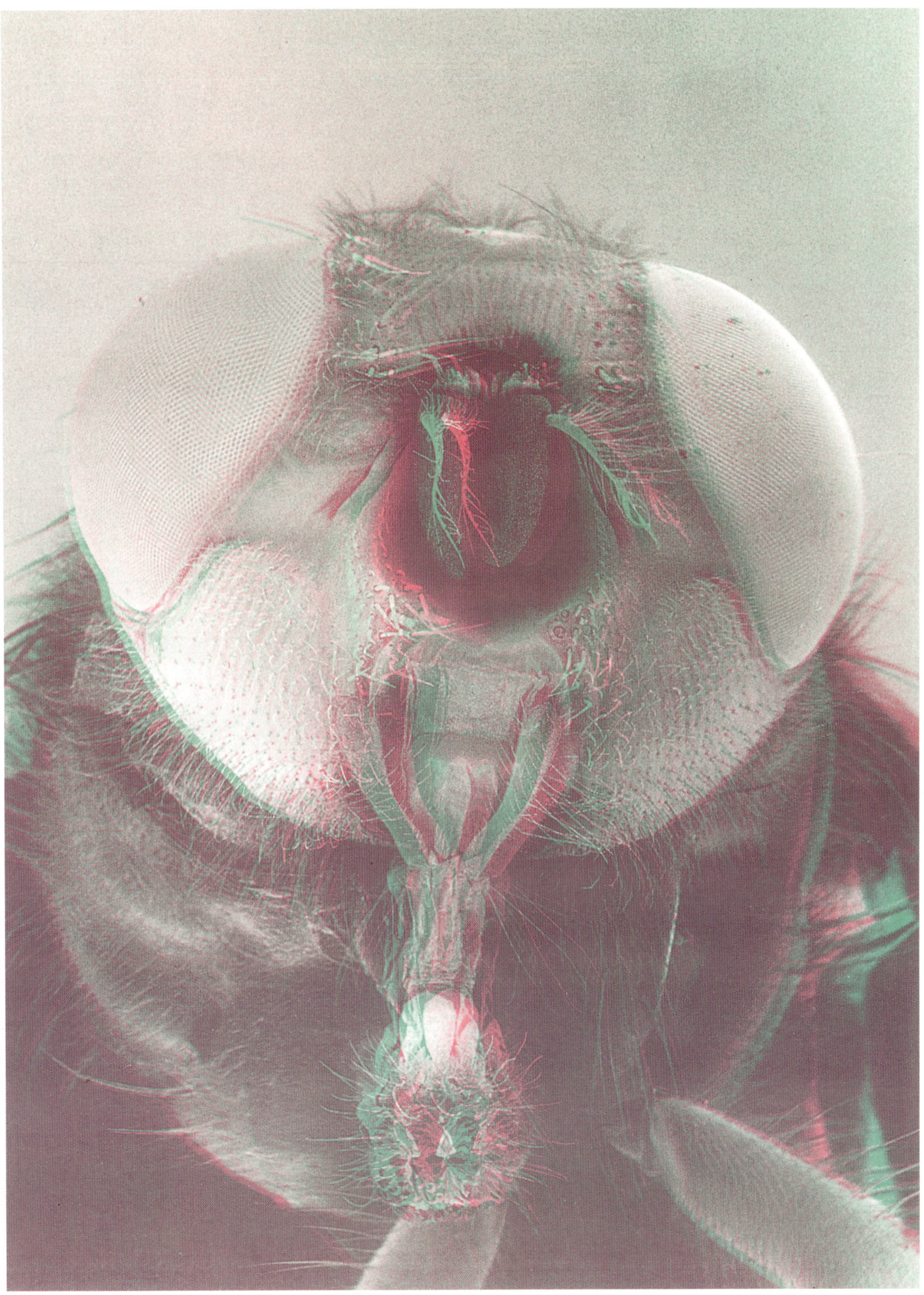

Parasites

Louse

Adult lice have a flattened body and strong claws for clinging onto hair or feathers, which makes them very hard to shake off. Their eggs (called nits) are also cemented firmly to fur or feather.

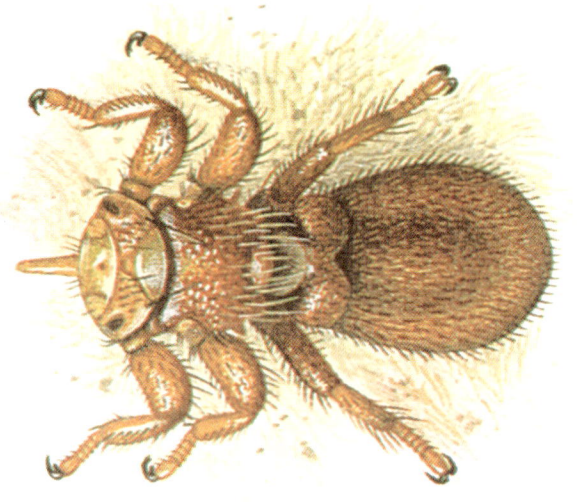

Bedbug

Blood-sucking bedbugs lurk in cracks and crevices until they sense a warm body nearby. They can live for up to a year without a meal.

FACT FILE

Nest flea

Practically every warm-blooded animal has its own special flea. Most fleas do not spend all - or even most - of their time riding on their victim.

As a larva, a flea scavenges debris in its host's nest. Cat and dog fleas then change into pupae which do not 'hatch' until they sense vibration and warmth.

Bird fleas, like this one, spend the winter as larvae. When the warm weather comes they mature into adults and wait for a bird to return, which is one good reason for leaving that old bird's-nest outside! It is also a good reason for cleaning out nest-boxes during the winter.

Cat flea

Cat fleas like warmth. Many fleas on modern pampered dogs are now cat-fleas. Their shiny white eggs slip into crevices, where they hatch into scavenging larvae that feed on nest debris. The pupae can survive for months, and can then 'hatch' in a moment as soon as a warm body comes close.

Earwigs & 'Roaches

Cicada

Although noisy, cicadas are not related to crickets. Their 'voice' comes from four chambers underneath the body. Technically classified as bugs, some of their nearest relatives are leafhoppers.

FACT FILE

Earwig
Earwigs do not creep inside peoples' ears. They may have got their name from their habit of creeping inside the 'ears' of plants. Earwigs climb up any stem to feed on the flower on top, so they can easily be trapped in a flowerpot balanced upside-down on a stick.
Earwig pincers look worse than they are. The male's curved pair can pinch but they cannot pierce human skin; a female's pincers are nearly straight and cannot even pinch properly.
There are about 1100 species of these fascinating insects worldwide, which are the only creatures of their kind on the face of the Earth.

Cockroach

Because they like warmth, and because they eat more-or-less what we eat, roaches have travelled around the world with people. This American cockroach can also be found in Europe.

Earwigs

Beneath those short wing-cases, earwigs pack a pair of large, gauzy wings. On warm nights, earwigs can fly as well as run.

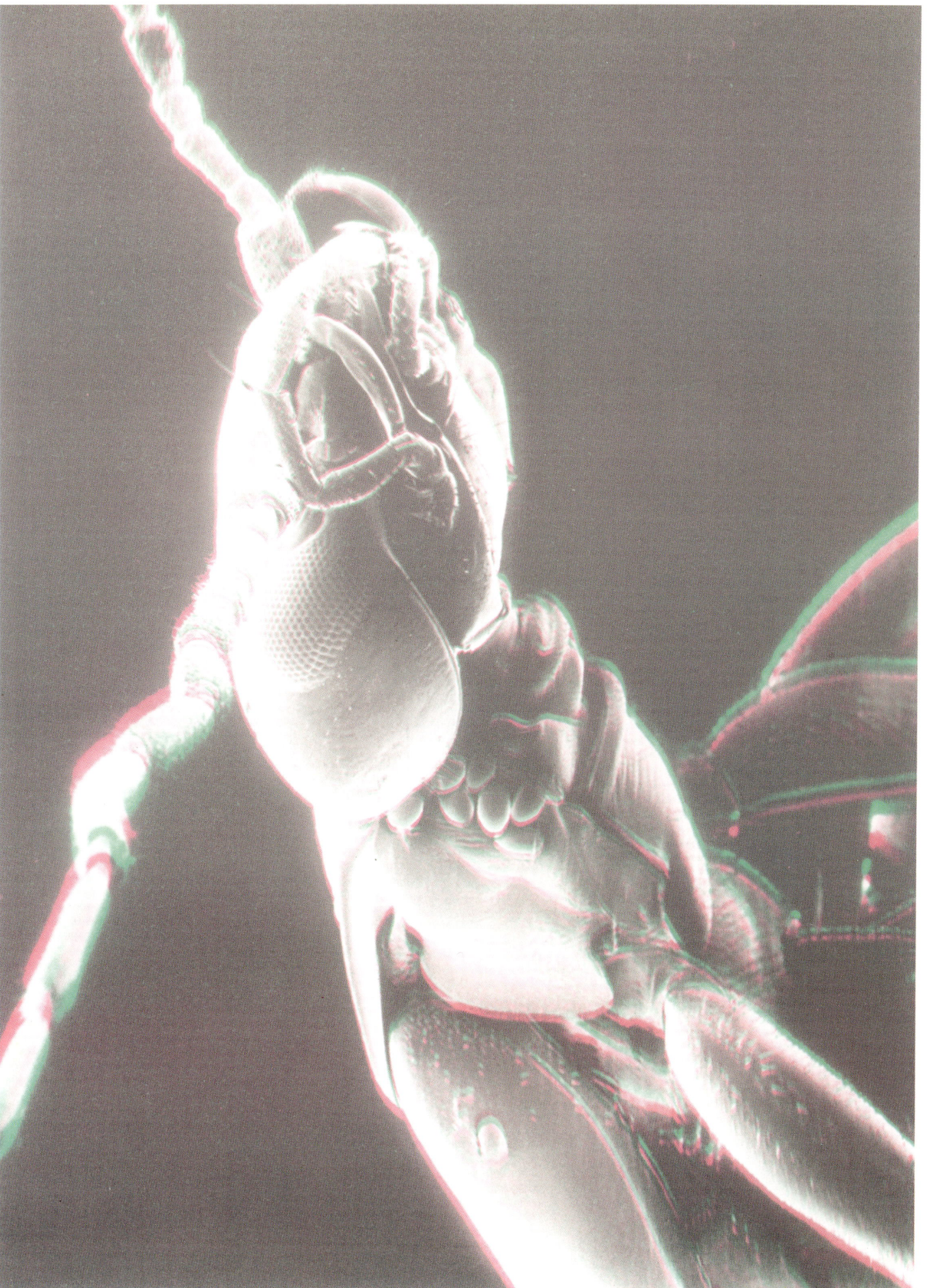

Frighteners

Diving spider

Dolomedes lives around the edges of ponds and streams and hunts in the water. It can carry enough air trapped in hairs on its body to allow it to dive underwater, and sometimes even catches small fish.

FACT FILE

Dust mite

Spiders may be obviously scary, but this microscopic mite probably causes more problems for more people than all the spiders in the world.
Our centrally-heated homes contain millions of dust-mites, feeding quietly on any scraps of organic matter they can scavenge, such as human skin scales or invisible crumbs from our table. The number of dust-mites living in an old mattress would have too many noughts to fit in this space. The problems come from dust-mite droppings, even smaller than the mites themselves, which can cause asthma, hay-fever and catarrh. Although the dust-mites can be destroyed by pesticides, or by keeping an infested item in a domestic freezer for several hours, their droppings can survive this treatment.

Red-kneed tarantula

Tarantulas are spectacular spiders. These large, hairy beasts are placid and not dangerous, although they may bite when startled. This species, which comes from Mexico, is a popular pet. So many red-kneed tarantulas have been captured for the pet trade, in fact, that they are now a protected species.

Suckers

Plant bug
Plant bugs have a stabbing mouth to pierce leaves and stems and suck the sap. They can also stab people.

Mosquito
A female mosquito waits for nightfall in a typical position. She will detect her prey by sensing a combination of body-warmth, carbon dioxide and some specific odours.

Horsefly
The bloodsucker with the beautiful eyes. Different species of horseflies can be recognised by the different patterns on their eyes. These iridescent colours disappear after the fly dies.

FACT FILE
Mosquito

Male mosquitoes have feathery antennae and females have straight ones. Only the females suck blood – they must have a blood meal before they can lay their eggs. Mosquito eggs are laid on the surface of stagnant water. Although the larvae develop and grow underwater, they do not have gills and need to come to the surface to breathe air.

Mosquitoes are feared because their bite spreads malaria, a disease that has defeated armies and killed countless numbers of people throughout history. It is still a deadly danger to travellers and people who live in warm, wet parts of the world.

One way to control malaria mosquitoes is by covering the surface of the water where they breed with a substance (such as oil) that prevents the larvae from breathing.

Wasp waists

Ants

We normally see small females called workers foraging for food. The larger queens stay inside the nest, laying eggs. Once a year, winged males emerge to pursue virgin queens.

Bees

Not all bees live in large colonies like honeybees. Many bees raise a family all alone.

FACT FILE

Ichneumon

Ichneumon 'wasps' have no nest to defend and no sting in their tail. The sting, known as an ovipositor, has become a tube for laying eggs inside another living organism.

Some members of this family, called sawflies, can drill a hole in the trunk of a tree to deposit an egg deep inside, where the larva will feed on wood for a year or two.

Many ichneumon wasps lay their eggs inside other larvae, such as caterpillars. As the caterpillar feeds and grows, the larvae eat the caterpillar from the inside. Finally, instead of the caterpillar turning into a chrysalis, many small ichneumon pupae emerge and the caterpillar dies.

Wasp nest

Common wasps build a paper nest by gnawing soft wood and mixing it with saliva. Each cell in the nest contains a larva, which is reared on chewed-up insects. Wasps are useful hunters for most of the year.

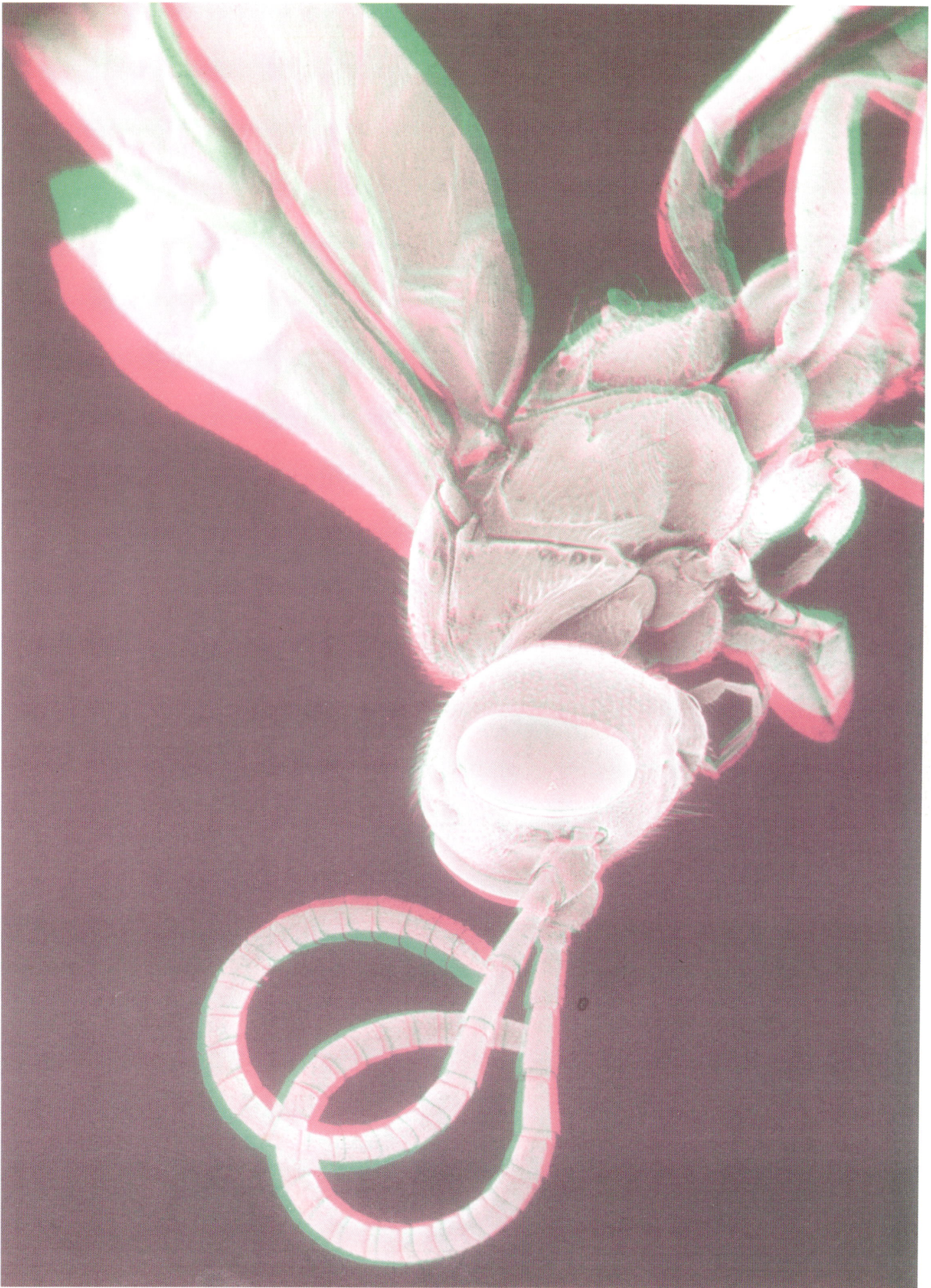

Spiders

Web Spider
A web-spider sets a snare for prey. It has very poor eyesight and finds the struggling insect by sensing vibrations in the web, picking its own way between the sticky threads to collect the living meal.

Jumping Spider
An active hunter, the jumping spider stalks by sight and stealth. Some very small species prey on creatures as tiny as springtails; some tropical species grow large enough to snatch frogs and birds.

Running repairs
After the prey has been dealt with, a web-spider busily mends its invisible trap. Spider silk is a form of protein manufactured and distributed from organs called spinnerets at the tip of its abdomen.

FACT FILE
Wolf spider
Although more difficult to spot than spiders sitting in a web, hunting spiders are commoner than most people realise. One pair of a wolf spider's eyes are much larger than the rest. They face forwards, as our own eyes do, so that the spider can judge distance accurately enough to make a strike with its first pounce. Once a spider has its hollow fangs embedded in any part of its victim's body, there is no escape. Fast-acting poisons paralyse the prey, which is then either wrapped in a silken parcel for later use or slowly eaten alive on the spot. Because wolf spiders do not build a web, they carry their eggs in a cocoon beneath their body. This is when they are easiest to find.

Beetles

Tiger Beetle

This beetle is an active hunter. Its giant serrated jaws are used to snap up its prey.

FACT FILE

Pea Beetle

There are probably more than 300,000 species of beetles in the world. They live everywhere except in the sea, and could be the most successful animals that ever evolved.

This little pea beetle is a larder pest. Before people started harvesting and storing peas, it was probably just another insect – like the Colorado beetle – with special dietary needs.

Pea beetles are sometimes called weevils because their larvae live inside dried foods and bore their way out when they are mature.

True weevils have a longer snout, with a tiny drilling mouth at the front.

Glow-worm

This glow-worm larva will become a beetle which uses flashing lights to attract a mate. The glow-worm's light comes from a chemical reaction between oxygen and a substance called luciferin. The reaction is so efficient that 98 per cent of the energy is emitted as light.

Colorado Beetle

Colorado beetles were once fairly rare leaf-beetles which lived on a plant called buffalo bur in the Rocky Mountains. When potatoes were planted nearby, the beetles changed their diet slightly and have now become a dreaded pest.

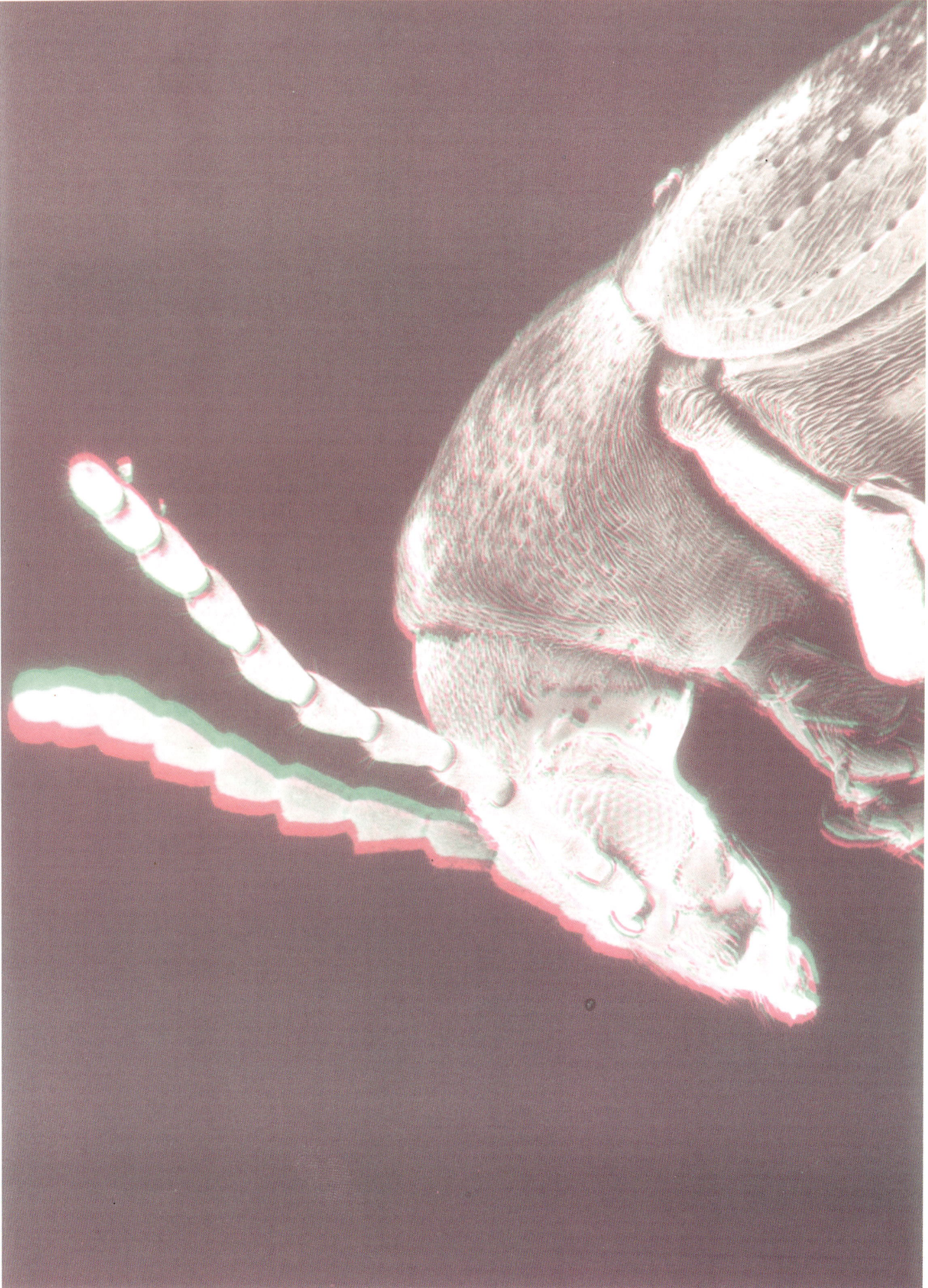

Legs

Centipede

The most common centipedes have around 30 legs, but some do have more than a hundred.

Their front legs carry poisoned claws that can paralyse prey larger than the centipede itself. A centipede's 'bite' is also painful to people.

FACT FILE

Millipede

Unlike centipedes, millipedes are peaceful vegetarians. They can only eat very soft or rotting plants.

No millipede has a thousand legs. But each body segment carries two pairs of legs, and a millipede grows more segments as it grows older, so a long millipede might have as many as two hundred legs.

Millipedes are not totally defenceless. They have scent glands that manufacture hydrocyanic acid, which is a very powerful poison gas. But the amount of the chemical each centipede makes is very small, so it probably works to repel enemies rather than kill them.

Woodlouse

Woodlice and pillbugs are among the few crustaceans (shellfish) that can survive on land. They still breathe with gills, which is why they need moisture to survive.

The gills are situated underneath the water-proof plates of the 'shell', and it is here that a female woodlouse also rears her young, in a moisture-filled sac, until they can survive on dry land by themselves.

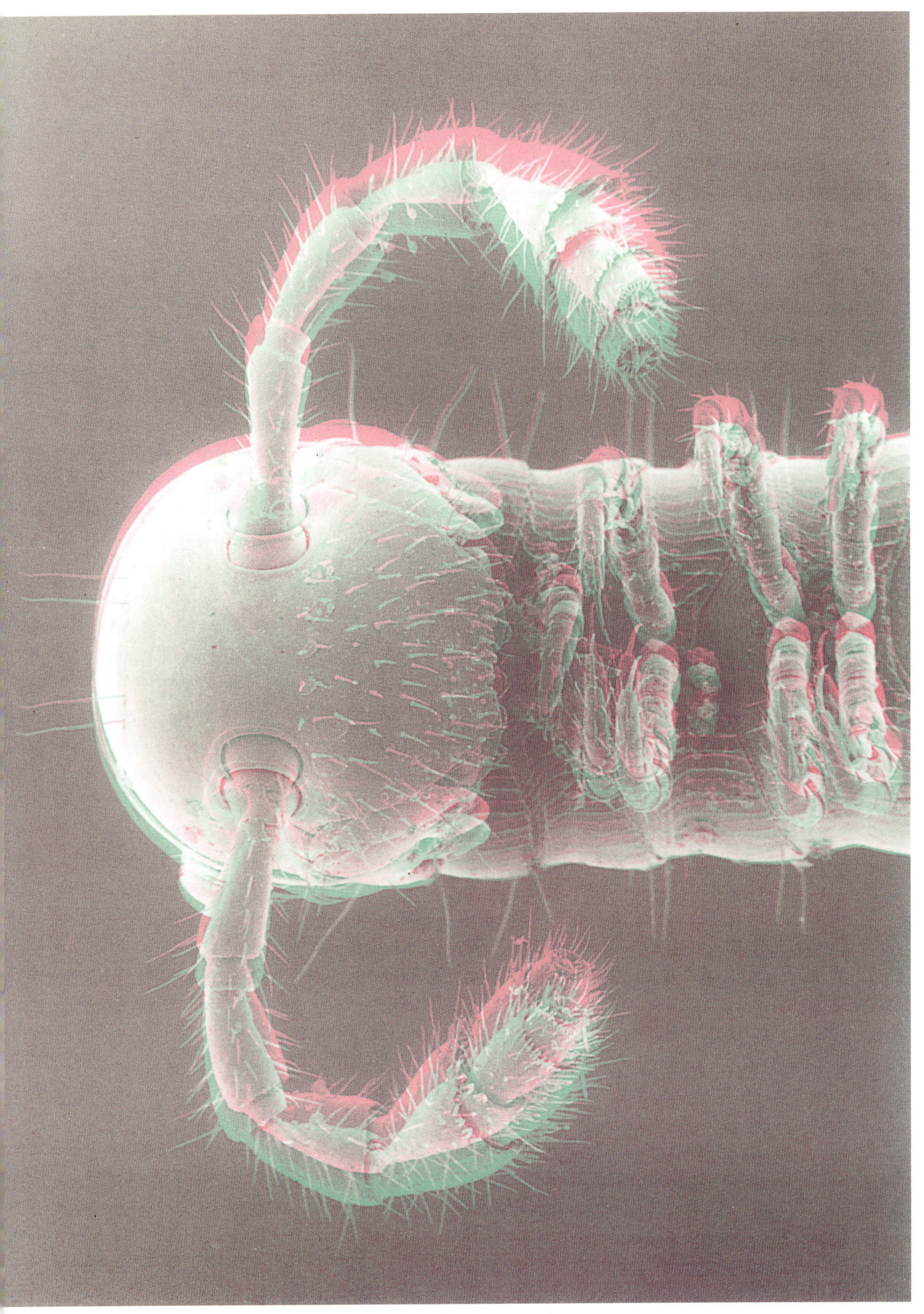

Primitives

Dragonfly

Giant fossil dragonflies with a wingspan of nearly a metre have been found in Carboniferous forests

Silverfish

Wingless silverfishes might be some of the most ancient insects in the world. They live on any kind of organic debris they can find, including fragments of skin left behind in the bath .

Praying mantis

Not praying, but waiting to lash out those folded arms to grab a passing insect. Mantises are related to roaches and stick-insects.

FACT FILE

Springtail

Perhaps the most abundant insects in the world, tiny primitive springtails are found from Pole to Pole. Wingless, and never more than a few millimetres long, they are named for the spring-loaded forked tail which enables them to leap 20 or 30 times as high as their own length. Most of the 1500 known species, including the springtails that live in leaf-litter and compost in our gardens, normally feed on decaying vegetation. Unusually for insects, some species survive and thrive in floating masses on tidal waters. Others manage to exist on mountain snow over permanent glaciers, but what they find to eat there is a mystery.

Springtails themselves are eaten by small predators, which are in turn eaten by larger predators. They are therefore a very important part of many foodchains.

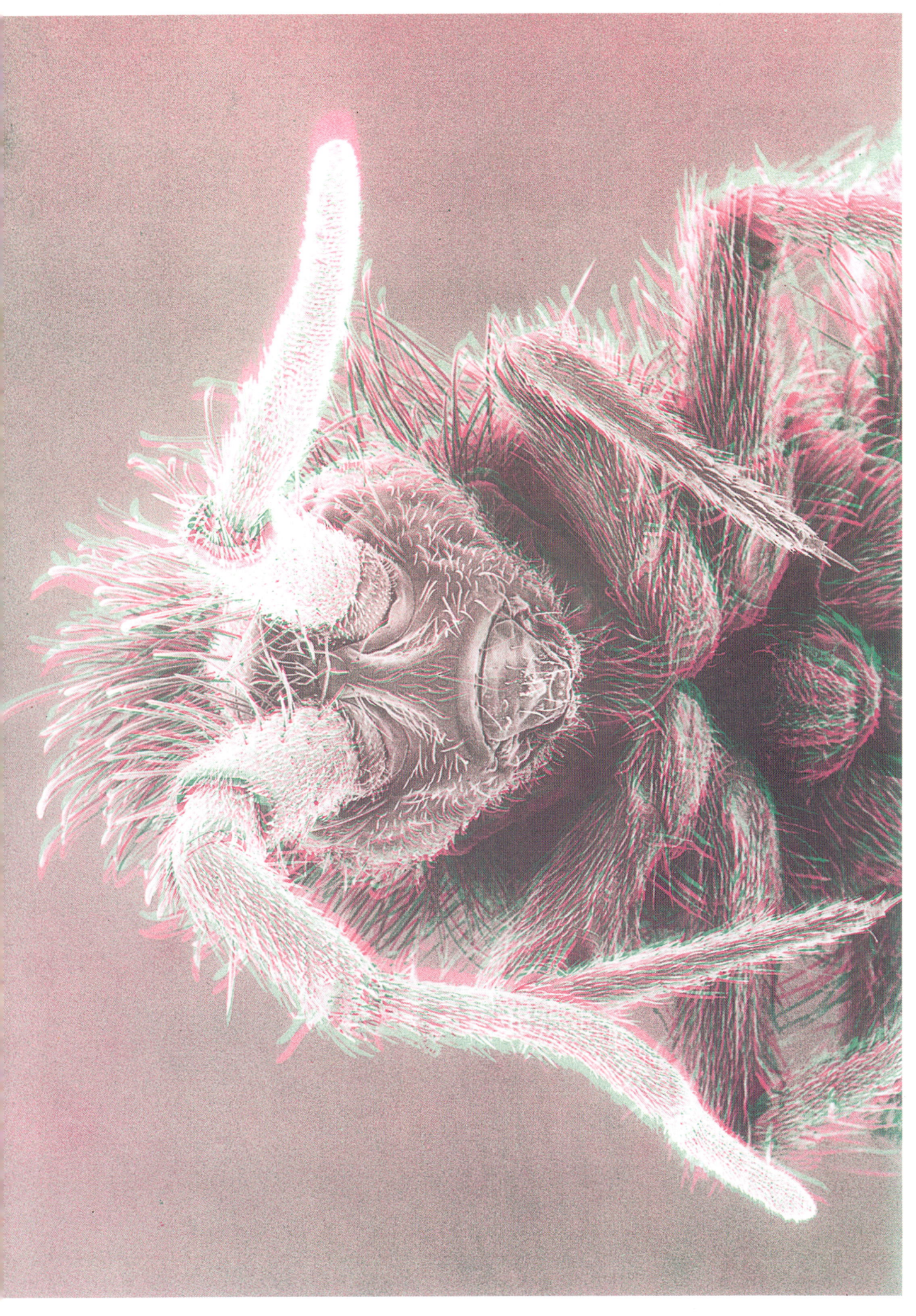

Other titles in this 3D series:

Incredible 3D Dinosaurs

  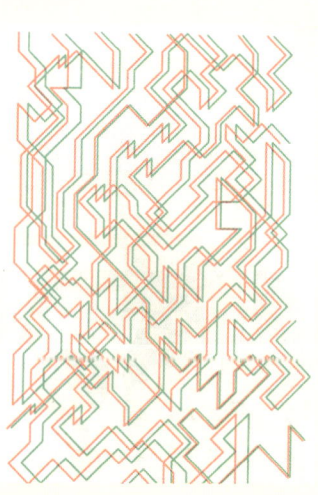

Optical Illusion 3D Puzzles

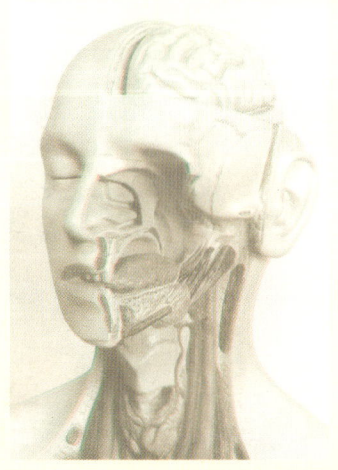 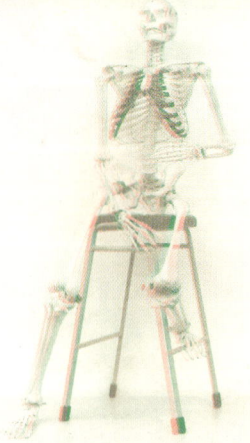 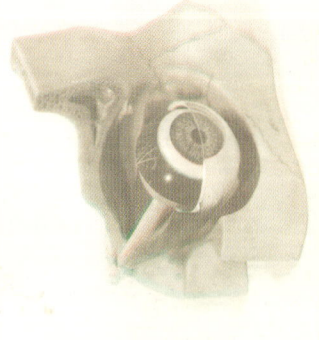

Human Body in Amazing 3D